TEACH YOURSELF
PIANO

by Mike Sheppard and James Sleigh

ISBN 97 -0-634-06979-6

HAL•LEONARD® CORPORATION

7777 W. BLUEMOUND RD. P.O. BOX 13819 MILWAUKEE, WI 53213

In Australia Contact:
Hal Leonard Australia Pty. Ltd.
22 Taunton Drive P.O. Box 5130
Cheltenham East, 3192 Victoria, Australia
Email: ausadmin@halleonard.com

Visit Hal Leonard Online at
www.halleonard.com

TEACH YOURSELF TO PLAY
PIANO

Contents

Introduction
So, you want to play piano?

Read this first

Well, the good news is that with a little perseverance and effort, and the help of this book, you'll find that learning the basics of piano playing is both fun and immensely rewarding. However, like all good things, if you want to enjoy the lifelong benefits and pleasure of playing the piano, you'll need commitment and a willingness to practice.

This book assumes no prior knowledge of the piano, or of music notation. We'll start from the most basic elements, building up slowly until you are playing complete tunes that will delight and impress your friends and family.

But I don't have a piano!

Acoustic pianos are expensive pieces of furniture, and you may be reluctant to invest in one right from the start. Fortunately, there are many affordable electronic keyboards which will allow you to learn the basics of piano playing. More expensive models will look a great deal like a piano, and may even have 'weighted' keys like a piano, but all the exercises and tunes in this book can be played on a simple keyboard with a three octave range.

Most keyboards also include a headphone socket, which will allow you to practice without annoying your neighbors, and are light and portable, which means that going on vacation isn't an excuse for not practicing!

Once you've covered the basic techniques explained in this book, you may well decide to invest in a traditional acoustic piano; we recommend that you make this investment if you are serious about becoming a pianist—the sooner your fingers get used to the feel of a real piano, the better. If you're nervous about investing in your own piano, many music shops also offer rental programs.

If you're lucky enough already to own an upright or grand piano, what are you waiting for? Let's get started!

Good foundations

Before we even play a note, let's spend a little time considering how to sit at the piano. It's vital to get into good habits right from the start; bad posture and body position will cause problems for you later, and they're much more difficult to unlearn once they've become ingrained.

First, find a good, comfortable seat. Piano stools are ideal, because they can be lowered or raised to accommodate players of different heights, but don't worry if you don't have one—just choose a comfortable chair and place it in front of your keyboard or piano. Sit on the chair and rest your hands on the keyboard. Your hands, wrists and elbows should be roughly in a straight line, horizontal, and parallel to the floor.

> **Seat too low:**
> Your wrists will be higher than your elbows
> **Seat too high:**
> Your elbows will be higher than your wrists.

Experiment with moving the chair closer and further away from the keyboard until your arms feel comfortable. In the early stages of learning you may be tempted to sit very close to the keyboard; resist this temptation, because as you progress to more challenging pieces it will start to become a problem.

> **Seat too close:**
> Your elbows will come out to the sides and your wrists will no longer be perpendicular to the keyboard.
> **Seat too far away:**
> Your arms will be too stretched.

If your keyboard or piano has pedals, make sure that your feet can reach them comfortably. We won't be using the pedals in this book, but later on you will want to use them, so make sure your playing position will allow you to do so.

Lastly, put this book on the music stand of your piano and make sure that it is roughly at eye level and that you can read the music examples comfortably. You should try to practice in an area with good light (preferably natural light), where you don't have to strain to read the music, or the text. If you wear glasses or contact lenses, it's also worth having your eyes retested to ensure that you have the correct lenses for reading at this distance.

As you work through the first few exercises in the book, you will need to look at your hands a lot to figure out where you are on the keyboard. However, your ultimate aim should always be to get to the stage where you can play without looking at your hands. Just like a good typist, a pianist needs to be able to keep his or her eyes on the music, without constantly looking up and down at the keyboard.

How to teach yourself

Working from a book like this one will require commitment, self-discipline and a lot of enthusiasm, but it will work. Each of the music examples has been carefully graded to introduce new concepts and techniques. Therefore, it's vital to master each exercise before you progress on to the next one. Don't be tempted to rush through the early exercises until you are really secure, because they provide the foundation for everything that follows.

How to practice

You may have come across other music books that promise to teach you how to play piano in a week, a day, or even an hour! Needless to say, very few people ever manage to make such rapid progress. However, if you can commit yourself to practicing for just 10 minutes every day, then you should be able to work through this book in four to six weeks.

Remember that it is much, much better to practice for a short time every day than it is to practice for several hours once a week. Choose one particular time and then try to practice at that time every day. It could be first thing in the morning, after breakfast, or perhaps later in the afternoon, when you get back from school or work. It doesn't really matter when you choose to practice, as long as you make a habit of it, like brushing your teeth before you go to bed.

Many people think of practice as a chore or as a task that is to be avoided at all costs. Nothing could be further from the truth—practice sessions are an exciting time in which you can learn new skills (and get great satisfaction from doing so) and enjoy the experience of playing music.

What can I do if I get stuck?

Although we've taken extreme care throughout the book to explain musical concepts and ideas in the simplest possible way, it is possible that you may find one particular point in the book which you simply can't understand or grasp. Don't worry if this happens, it's entirely normal. The important thing is not to give up at this point; ask any musical friends that you may have for their input, get in touch with your local music school or teacher, or contact an Internet discussion group. There are thousands of people out there who have gone through the same learning process, and most of them would be delighted to help you out.

Do I need piano lessons?

Piano lessons can be an expensive option for the beginner (one lesson could easily cost you more than the price of this book). However, if, by the time that you have worked through this book, you decide that you want to develop further as a pianist, lessons are a worthy investment. A good piano teacher will be able to spot any bad habits that you have developed and correct them before you progress too far; not only that, but a regular piano lesson once a week is an ideal motivation to practice! A good teacher can be an inspiration, but a bad teacher could kill your piano playing ambitions; ask around in your local area for recommendations from other pupils. Remember, good teachers will be busy teachers!

A good place to start looking for piano teachers is your local music shop—check out their noticeboard or ask them if they keep a list of teachers in the area.

Ok! We're now ready to start learning about the piano keyboard.

Chapter 1
Familiarize yourself with the keyboard

An acoustic piano is a complex piece of machinery; lift up the lid and look inside and you'll see a complicated set of strings, hammers and dampers. Compare this to the relatively simple design of other musical instruments like the violin or the recorder and you could be forgiven for assuming that the piano was a complicated instrument to learn to play.

Nothing could be further from the truth; the purpose of all that machinery is to make life easier for the player. In fact, it's easier to produce a sound on the piano than on almost any other instrument. Try it yourself—press down any key and listen to the sound. Essentially, there's no difference between what you just did and what a concert pianist does during a professional recital. Try the same thing with a violin and you might not get such good results!

Let's take a moment to look closely at the keyboard:

The keyboard consists of black and white keys (these are actually levers that work the machinery inside the piano, propelling the hammer toward the string to create a sound). The most crucial thing to note at this stage is that there are repeating patterns of notes, which appear in exactly the same form across the keyboard. For example, the pattern of two black keys, followed by three black keys is repeated across the entire keyboard.

These patterns repeat at a fixed interval, called an octave. So, for example, the note marked '2' on the diagram above is said to be 'one octave' above the note marked '1' (and, conversely, note '1' is one octave below note '2').

Within each octave every note is given a name. All notes in the same place in the repeating pattern of black and white notes have the same name. For example, in the diagram above, notes '1' and '2' have the same name. This is very good news, because instead of having to remember hundreds of different note names, you only need to remember twelve.

Let's start with the white keys:

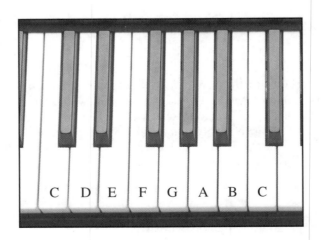

Each note is given a letter name, based on the first seven letters of the alphabet. Because there are only seven white keys before the pattern of notes repeats itself, we only need seven names. Once we reach G, we start again at A. So, for example, there's no such thing as the notes J, L and W! This means that every eighth note has the same name, hence the 'oct' in octave.

This repeating pattern of notes can be extended to cover the whole keyboard, as shown below:

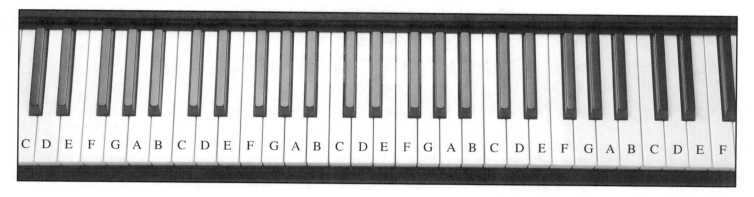

Practice finding notes in all octaves, across the whole keyboard. For example, find all the As or all the Cs and play them. Listen to the sound of each note as you play it and try to hear how notes with the same letter name sound similar.

A good way to help memorize the position of each note is to look out for the note C (which appears just to the left of the group of two black notes) and F (which can be found just to the left of the group of three black notes). These *marker notes* are easy to spot and you can then count up or down to find the note you're after:

Now cover the top half of this page and then write in the note names where indicated on the diagram below:

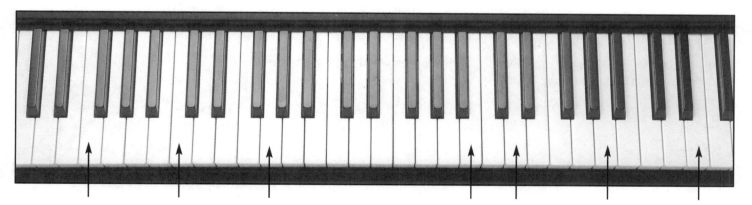

The black notes

At this stage, we don't need to worry about naming the black notes, as all the exercises in the first part of this book use only the white keys. However, it's worth knowing that the black keys are often referred to as *sharps* and *flats*.

Chapter 2
Playing your first notes

So, we've established that lots of different keys on the keyboard share the same names; for example, there might be six Cs across the whole range of your keyboard. In order to start playing we need to choose one note on the keyboard as a reference point, so that you know you're starting in the right place.

Traditionally, this reference note is known as *Middle C*. It's given this name because (you've guessed it) it's the C note nearest to the middle of the keyboard. On our keyboard, Middle C is shown below:

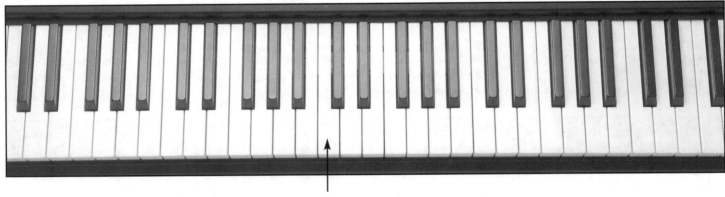

Middle C

Try to find Middle C on your keyboard. (If you have an acoustic piano, Middle C is often found just above the lock.)

Now place the thumb of your right hand on Middle C and press down the key. Congratulations! You've just played your first note as a pianist. Experiment with pressing the key down really softly and notice that this makes the sound of the note quieter; then try hitting the key really hard and listen out for the loud noise that it will create. This ability to make sounds of different volumes was revolutionary when the piano was invented, and it was immortalized in the name given to the instrument—*pianoforte*—or 'quiet-loud' in Italian.

Keep the thumb of your right hand on Middle C and let the other fingers of your hand fall naturally over the next four white notes to the right of Middle C.

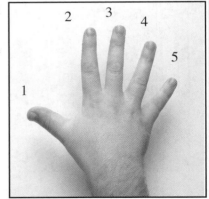

The diagram below shows exactly where your fingers should go, according to the numbering system shown on the right:

    1 = thumb
    2 = index finger
    3 = middle finger
    4 = ring finger
    5 = little finger

Once you've got your right hand in the correct position, experiment with playing different combinations of the five notes and listen to the sounds that you create. Try pressing down each key individually, without moving any of your other fingers—this will feel difficult to start with, but don't give up!

The five notes that you are playing are called C, D, E, F and G:

A great way to practice these five notes is to get a friend or family member to call out one of the five letter names; with your hand in position over the five notes, you can then try to play the right note. Remember to only use your thumb to play C, index finger to play D, middle finger to play E, and so on.

You're now well on the way to being able to play your first tune with the right hand. But before we do that we need to introduce music notation. This is the 'language' of music and provides a way for composers to communicate with musicians and let them know what to play. Once you can read music you will be able to understand (and hopefully, play) any piece of sheet music, and you'll be able to communicate with other musicians all over the world.

All music is written on five horizontal lines, called a *staff*. Here is an example of a staff:

Ignore the curly symbol at the start of the staff for a moment and concentrate on the five lines. These five lines provide a 'grid' on which we can plot notes. Low notes appear at the bottom of the grid, and high notes appear at the top of the grid.

So, in this example, the note on the left is lower than the note on the right. The grid also shows time—so in this example, the note on the left would be played *before* the note on the right.

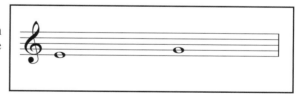

The five notes that you've just played—C, D, E, F and G—are represented on the staff like this. C, the lowest note, appears lowest on the staff, while G, the highest note, appears higher on the staff than any of the other notes. Notice also that the C 'hangs' under the five lines of the staff on its own, shorter line, known as a *ledger line*. When plotting notes on the staff we can use either the line itself, or the space between the lines, to indicate where a note lies. So, for example, the note F is found in the space between the bottom two lines, whereas E is found on the bottom line.

The curly symbol at the beginning of the staff is known as a *clef*, and is very useful, because it tells us exactly which lines on the staff correspond to which notes. This particular clef is called a *treble clef*, or *G clef*, because it curls around the line where we can find the note G.

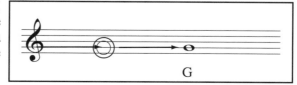

There are lots of neat ways of remembering which lines (and spaces) correspond to which notes. A favorite technique of musicians over the years has been to create a *mnemonic*; this is a phrase where the first letters of each word give the letter names of the notes. So for example, a mnemonic to remember the notes on the five lines of the staff might be 'Every Good Boy Does Fine.' The sillier they are the better—it will help you remember the note names.

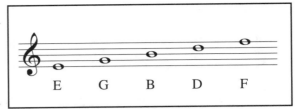

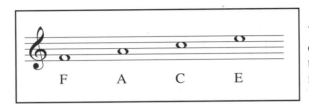

You can do exactly the same thing to remember the letter names of the spaces on the staff. This pattern is easy because it spells the word '**FACE**,' but once again, you can have a lot of fun making up your own mnemonic.

Use the examples below to test yourself until you're absolutely certain that you can name the notes from the staff, and find them on the keyboard. Answers are given on page 14. Start with this test: write down the letter names of these groups of notes under the staff—to make things slightly easier for you, each group of notes spells a word.

Now do the same thing in reverse; draw notes on the staff below according to the letter names written below the staff:

B   E   A   D   D   A   D   A   G   E   D   A   C   E

And finally, look at the keyboard diagram below, which has four notes marked on it. Write the letter names of these notes under the staff and then add the correct notes to the staff itself.

Chapter 3
Getting started with the right hand

You now know enough about the keyboard and music notation to start playing your first melodies.

Let's recap what you learned in the previous chapter. Here are the five notes that you found on the keyboard, with your thumb on Middle C:

This is how they are represented in musical notation. The number near each note tells you which finger to use to play it.

Sit down at your piano and play the notes shown below. Say the name of each note out loud as you play it, and try to play every note firmly and confidently.

One of the basic elements of music, which we haven't discussed yet, is *rhythm*. Rhythm is a vital part of almost all styles of music and, fortunately, music notation has a system to represent just about any rhythm you can think of. It does this through the shape and size of the noteheads themselves, and the different ways in which they can be connected together.

Look at the example below, which shows two notes on what should be, by now, a familiar staff:

Count: 1   2   3   4   1   2   3   4

This notehead looks like a slightly squashed circle and we've used it to indicate all the notes you've come across so far because it's the simplest type of notehead. Its proper name is a *whole note*, and in music notation it is given a rhythmic value of four beats.

Try playing the note above, and count slowly and steadily from one to four as you do so. When you get to four, start again at one, pressing the note down again as you do so. It's much more important to count steadily than it is to go quickly, so take it as slowly as you like.

Bars and beats

You may have noticed that in the previous music example there was a vertical line cutting across the five lines of the staff between the two notes. It's called a *barline*, and it's there to divide up the music into equal rhythmic sections (called *bars* or *measures*). Almost all music has a regular pulse that runs through it—we play along with this pulse when we tap our foot to a catchy tune or clap in time with the music. Musicians call this pulse the *beat,* and learning to feel it is a vital part of becoming a pianist.

In the previous example, once you'd counted from one to four, you started again at one. That marks the beginning of a new bar, and is shown on the staff by the appearance of the barline. This is described as 'counting four beats to the bar'.

As you work through the following examples, remember to count out loud from one to four, as rhythmically and steadily as you can. Don't worry if you have to start out very slowly; it's much better to play slowly and steadily than it is to play quickly and unrhythmically.

Let's try a very simple melody that uses only two notes. Put the thumb of your right hand on Middle C, and place your other fingers on the notes D, E, F and G, as shown below:

Now follow the music below, starting with your little finger. The numbers below the staff tell you which fingers to use:

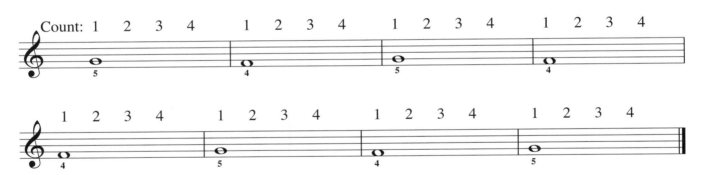

This is the first music example that you've seen that is longer than four bars. Music reads just like text, so when you get to the right hand end of the first line, move down to the next line of music, starting at the left hand side. There should be no pause in your counting as you move from one line to the next.

Let's introduce another note. Keep your right hand in exactly the same position, with the thumb on Middle C, and make sure you use the fingers as indicated below each note. Count firmly and steadily from one to four as you play.

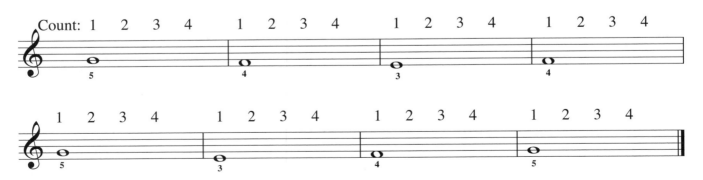

Don't be discouraged if you can't play this right away. Keep practicing, slowly and steadily, and you will gradually get better and better. Make sure you've mastered each exercise before you move on to the next one.

Correct hand position

As you're playing through these exercises, pay special attention to the position of your hand on the keyboard. In order to get the correct hand position, turn your right hand over so that your palm is facing upwards. Then imagine that you are holding a piece of fruit, like an orange or an apple. Keep your hand in that position and turn it over and place it on the piano keyboard. This is the correct playing position, as shown below:

Keep your arm and wrist relaxed and gently poised above the keys. When you press a key down the movement should come from the finger concerned—don't move the whole hand. Some time spent perfecting this now will save you hours later on, so be tough on yourself and don't let bad habits creep in!

Shown below are two common mistakes that beginners make. In the left hand photo, the pianist's fingers are far too flat; the tips of your fingers should be meeting the keyboard at right angles. In the right hand photo, the wrist has dropped right down below the level of the keys: the arm, wrist and hand should all be horizontal, above the keys.

Here's a fun exercise that will help your hand position.

Take a coin (it doesn't really matter what type) and hold it in your left hand. Put your right hand on the keyboard in the correct position and place the coin on the back of your right hand. As long as you keep your hand in the right position, the coin won't fall off. Try playing through the exercises in this chapter like this and see how long you can keep the coin in position!

Let's get back to some more melodies. Here's a tune that uses four notes:

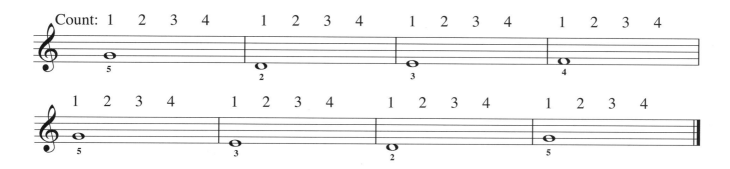

Look out for the leap between the first two notes and the last two. Try to look ahead as you play through the tune so that you're always prepared for what's coming next. Once again, count slowly and steadily and make sure you use the fingers shown under each note.

Now here's a chance to play a tune using all five notes that you've learned so far.

This tune includes lots of different distances between notes (commonly called *intervals*), so pay attention!

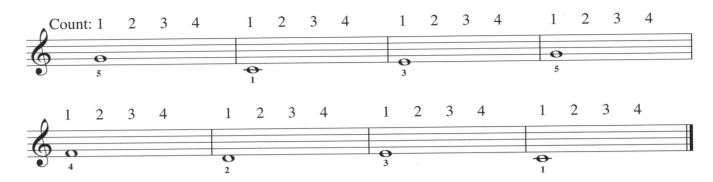

Finally, try this tune. We've removed the 1-2-3-4 count and the fingering from this example, but you should keep counting and aim to use one finger per note, just as you did in the example above.

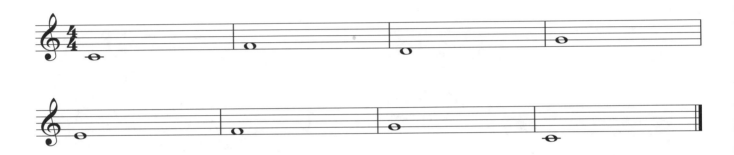

Five note checklist

Here's a checklist of things to think about as you practice these pieces:

• Count slowly and steadily.

• Don't try to run before you can walk! Start slowly and speed up gradually.

• Make sure you use the fingerings shown under each note—where fingerings aren't given, write your own in and make sure you stick to them!

• Look ahead so that you know what's coming up.

Quiz answers from page 10

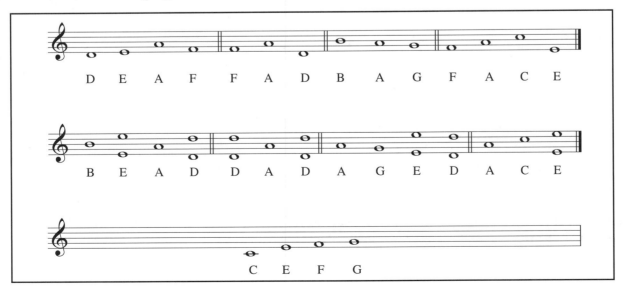

Chapter 4
Get rhythm!

So far, all the notes you've played have been the same length—four beats. Now we're going to look at a different type of note; it's called the *quarter note*, and (surprise, surprise) it's a quarter of the length of a whole note. A whole note lasts for four beats, and a quarter note lasts for one beat.

This is what a quarter note looks like on the staff. Notice that this note has a vertical line attached to it—it's called a *stem*, and it can go up or down from the note, depending how high or low the note is on the staff.

Sound and silence

Ask any musician and they will tell you that the notes you *don't* play are just as important as the ones that you *do*!

Just as music notation has symbols to tell you when to play, it also has symbols to tell you when *not* to play. These symbols are called *rests,* and there is an equivalent rest for every type of note.

Here's the quarter note and its equivalent rest:

Try this exercise, which combines quarter notes and quarter note rests. You can either play through the exercise on the piano, or just clap each note. Count out loud as you do so:

You may have noticed that another symbol has appeared at the beginning of this exercise. Just after the treble clef, you will notice a symbol that looks like two fours stacked on top of one another. This is known as a *time signature*, and it tells musicians how many beats there are in each bar.

In this particular example, the top number tells us that each bar contains four beats, and the bottom number tells us that each beat is a quarter note.

Now let's try combining quarter notes with some of the five notes you learned in the previous chapter.

Try clapping through the exercise first, before you attempt to play it at the piano. As always, keep a very steady and slow rhythm, and build up speed gradually as you become more confident.

Here's another exercise for you to try. Make sure you let go of the notes that come before each rest, so that the sound of the note doesn't spill over into the rest.

15

The next exercise has even more rests. Once again, clap through the rhythm before you try to play it on the keyboard:

Look out for the last bar in particular—there's no note on the first beat of the bar, so watch out!

And here's one last exercise, to make sure that you have really mastered the quarter note and quarter note rest:

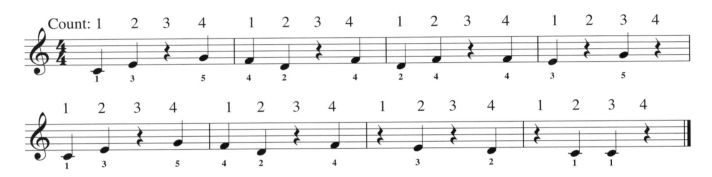

Again, the last two bars are a little bit tricky, so watch out! If you find that you're having particular difficulty with one bar or section of an exercise, then isolate that section and practice it on its own, really slowly. Keep working at it over and over again until you do it almost from memory. Then revert to practicing the whole exercise and you should find that the previously troublesome section is a lot easier.

Here are some tips to help you get a grip on quarter notes and rests:

- Rests are just as important as notes, and they deserve just as much attention.

- Clap out the rhythm of each piece before you try to play it.

- Isolate difficult sections and practice them separately.

- Start *really* slowly, and speed up as you gain confidence.

- Use a metronome. This is a musical device designed to keep perfect time. Although originally a mechanical invention, affordable electronic versions are now available. Simply set the metronome to a slow speed (start at around 60 beats per minute) and listen to the audible beeps or clicks. Play along and increase the speed as you gain in confidence.

As a final test, try this short piece. We've removed the 1-2-3-4 count and the fingering, but that doesn't mean that you should stop counting! Try writing in your own fingering as you practice.

Chapter 5
Introducing the Bass Clef

Up to this point, your left hand hasn't had a great deal to do, other than clapping out a few quarter note rhythms. That's all about to change, however, as we start to investigate the wonderful world of the bass clef.

By now, you should be familiar with your right hand position, with the thumb on Middle C and the other fingers covering the notes of D, E, F and G. Now look to the left of this position and find the C an octave below Middle C, as shown below:

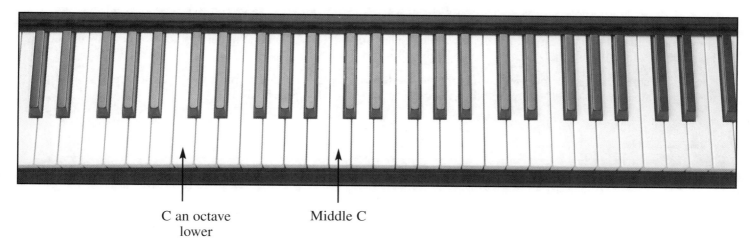

C an octave   Middle C
lower

Once you've found this note, put the little finger of your left hand on it, and spread the other four fingers over the next four white keys, as shown below:

The finger numbering system for the left hand is a mirror image of that for the right hand:

    1 = thumb
    2 = index finger
    3 = middle finger
    4 = ring finger
    5 = little finger

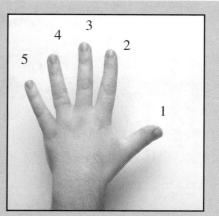

All the comments on right hand position also apply to the left hand; the fingers should be curled over, the back of the hand should be flat, wrist straight, and the whole arm should be relaxed.

If necessary, use the 'coin on the back of the hand' technique to ensure that you have the correct position.

Your left hand is now in exactly the same position as your right hand, except that it's an octave lower. That means that your five fingers are covering exactly the same five letter names: C, D, E, F and G:

So, how does music notation represent these new notes? They're a lot lower than the five notes you've played with the right hand, so they won't fit onto the staff that we've been using so far.

We need to create a new staff to represent notes that the left hand plays. Don't worry, though, as it's very similar to the staff that you already know, although the notes themselves appear in different positions:

The first thing you'll notice is that we still have five horizontal lines on which the various notes sit. But the curly symbol at the start of the staff has changed—this new symbol is called the *bass clef*, or *F clef*.

Just like the treble clef (or G clef), the bass clef tells us which lines correspond to which notes. In this case the 'blob' at the center of the clef is sitting on the second line from the top of the staff, and it tells us that this line represents the note F. By filling in the other lines and spaces, we can then plot the notes C, D, E and G, as above.

Confusion alert!

You may already have noticed that, for example, a C on the bass clef appears in a different place to C on the treble clef. In fact, all the notes are in different places, which is potentially rather confusing!

There are historical and practical reasons for this difference, but unfortunately space doesn't allow for a full explanation here. For the time being, you will just have to accept that that's the way it is. Fortunately, the same strategies we used to memorize the notes on the treble staff will also help here.

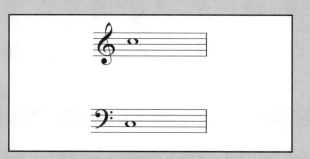

Once again *mnemonics* are a really useful way to learn the names of the notes on the staff. For notes on the lines, how about using:

Good **B**oys **D**o **F**ine **A**lways

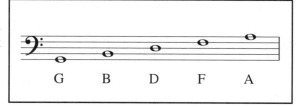

G B D F A

A C E G

For the spaces, you could try:

All **C**ows **E**at **G**rass

Feel free to make up your own, even more ludicrous, examples.

18

Use the examples below to test yourself until you're absolutely certain that you can name the notes from the staff, and find them on the keyboard. Answers are given on page 28. Write down the letter names of these groups of notes under the staff—to make things slightly easier for you, each group of notes spells a word:

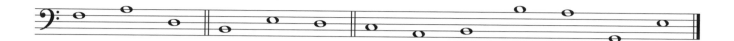

Now do the same thing in reverse; draw notes on the staff below according to the letter names written below the staff:

A   D   A   G   E   D   E   A   D   C   A   G   E

And finally, look at the keyboard diagrams below, which have four notes marked on them. Write the letter names of these notes under the staves and then add the correct notes to the staves themselves.

Chapter 6
Getting started with the left hand

Let's recap what you learned in the previous chapter. Here are the five notes that you found with your left hand, with your little finger on the C below Middle C:

And this is how they are represented in musical notation:

Sit down at your piano and pick out the notes shown below with your left hand. Say the name of each note out loud as you play it, and try to play every note firmly and confidently.

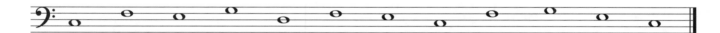

Now try playing this simple bass melody, which only uses two notes:

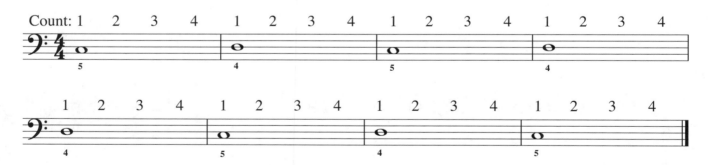

Next, try this example, which uses three different notes:

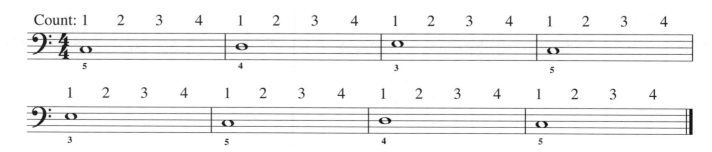

20

This example adds the note F to the C, D, and E from the previous example:

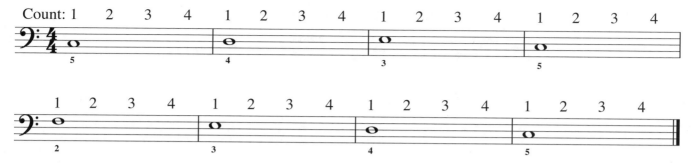

And finally, this example uses all five notes, from C to G:

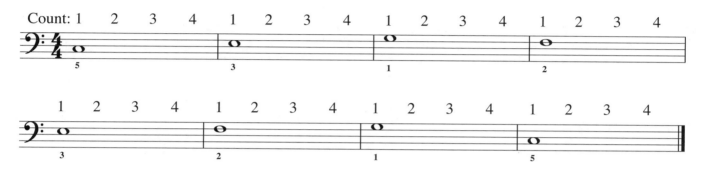

The left hand and quarter notes

In Chapter 4 we introduced the quarter note and quarter note rest and you used them to play several different melodies. Now we can do the same thing with the left hand:

This tune uses all five notes from the left hand, and a selection of quarter notes and rests. As always, clap through the rhythm of the tune before you attempt to play it, counting out loud:

Now let's put everything together. This exercise uses whole notes, quarter notes and quarter note rests and will really give your left hand a good workout! As before, make sure that you release each quarter note exactly on the next beat, so that they don't continue sounding over the rests. Look out for the very final rest at the end of the last bar—make sure you release the final C with your little finger exactly on the count of '4'. This will give a very definite ending to the piece.

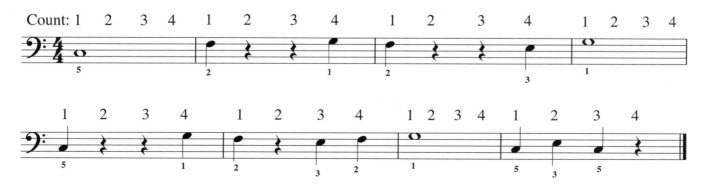

Chapter 7
Introducing the eighth note

Now it's time to introduce another note value, which will mean that you can start playing some really interesting melodies.

So far, you've encountered the whole note (which is held for four beats) and the quarter note (one beat). The next note value that we're going to look at is the *eighth note*. Those of you with a mathematical brain will probably already have worked out that an eighth note is worth half of a quarter note—or to look at it another way, one quarter note equals two eighth notes.

Just like the quarter note, the eighth note has an equivalent rest; this is what they look like on the staff:

Like the quarter note, the eighth note has a vertical line attached to it, but it also has a small 'squiggle' attached to the end of the stem, called a *flag*. When two or more eighth notes appear together, these flags can be joined to form a *beam*. This doesn't change the way that the notes are played, it just makes them neater on the page, and therefore easier to read.

Counting the eighth note

So, we know that eighth notes last for half the time that quarter notes do—in other words, they go by twice as fast.

We need to find a way of counting beats that will allow us to subdivide each beat into two. Fortunately there is a very simple way of doing this, as the example below demonstrates:

Play or clap the simple quarter note rhythm as shown above. Count the first bar as normal, but when you reach the second bar, add the word 'and' in between each number as you count. Keep the same pulse going and just squeeze the extra word in the gap between the numbers—each bar should still last for the same amount of time as before.

Now try the same exercise again, but this time, when you count 'one and two and three and four and,' clap or play along with every word. If necessary, use a metronome to keep your counting even:

Remember this only happens in bars two and four; bars one and three remain the same as before.

You can use the 'and method' any time you need to count an eighth note, no matter where it appears in the bar. Try the example below, which combines eighth and quarter notes within the same bar:

22

Before you try the next exercise, read out the count above the staff as rhythmically as you can. Then clap or play the rhythms, looking out for the eighth notes throughout:

play or clap

The next three exercises have different combinations of quarter notes and eighth notes and their respective rests.

play or clap

play or clap

play or clap

Rhythm plus notes equals fun!

Now you have a great selection of rhythms to use, so we can start to play melodies that sound really good.

Try this one out to start with:

Notice that we've stopped putting finger numbers under every note. Most sheet music doesn't show fingerings unless they differ from what you would normally expect to find. So, in this case, keep your right hand in its usual five-finger position with the thumb on Middle C, and all the notes will fall under those five fingers. Don't be tempted to move your hand out of this position, as you could find that you don't have enough fingers left to finish the tune!

Here's a more jaunty melody for you to try:

As before, if you have trouble understanding the rhythms, start by reading out the count above the staff as rhythmically as possible. Once you've mastered that, then add in the notes *very* slowly. It doesn't matter how slowly you play to start with as long as you play steadily and rhythmically.

Left hand melodies

There's no reason why the left hand can't join in the fun as well. As with the right hand examples on the previous page, we've omitted the fingering from these tunes. However, they can all be played in the five-finger position that you've already learned, with your little finger on the C below Middle C.

Try this one: (Look out for the big jumps in bars 1 and 4—these are a typical feature of many bass lines.)

This example combines smooth runs of notes in bars 1 and 3 with big jumps in bars 2 and 4:

The next tune has a more 'classical' feel to it—enjoy the run of notes in the last bar:

Finally, try this example, which consists entirely of eighth notes:

This type of bass pattern is known as an 'Alberti' bass part, and was frequently used by composers like Haydn and Mozart. Try to keep the eighth notes as even as you can, and don't rush–keep counting steadily as you play and you shouldn't have any problems.

Eighth note tips

The eighth note is the shortest (and therefore, quickest) note that you've learned so far, and it will enable you to play many more exciting rhythms and melodies. Follow these hints and tips to get a grip on the eighth note:

- Use the 'and method' to count any eighth notes you come across.
- Count each piece before you try to play it.
- Don't forget, rests are just as important as notes, so look out for them.
- Practice really, really slowly until you are confident in what you are playing.
- Try always to play eighth notes evenly and steadily. There will always be a temptation to rush them—resist this by counting aloud as you play. If necessary, use a metronome.

Chapter 8
Hands together

In this chapter you're going to get your first chance to play using both hands. But before we do that, there's one more note value to introduce to you.

Once again, those of you with a talent for math may have realized that there a gap in our family of note values. We've already encountered whole notes, quarter notes and eighth notes, so the missing note value is *half notes*.

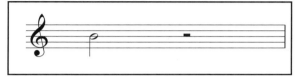

As you may guessed, a half note is half the length of a whole note, and twice the length of a quarter note. Just like all the other note values, the half note has an equivalent rest and this is what they look like on the staff:

The half note looks like a cross between the whole note and the quarter note; its note head is not filled in like the whole note, but it has a stem like the quarter note. Try playing or clapping along as you count:

Here's another example, featuring plenty of half note rests—make sure that you let go of the previous note on time so that there is complete silence for the duration of the rest:

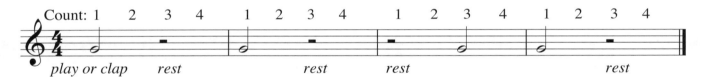

Our family of note values can now be summarized like this.

Each note value can be halved to get the next shortest note value, or doubled to get the next longest.

Also included here is the equivalent rest for the whole note. It's easily confused with the half note rest; the half note rest sits *on* the third line of the staff, while the whole note rest *hangs from* the fourth line.

One way of remembering the difference is to think that it is harder to hang onto something than it is to sit on something; therefore, the rest hanging from the line is longer than the one sitting on the line.

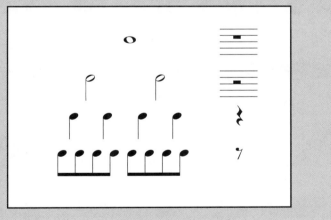

Now it's time to take everything you've learned so far and apply it to both hands together...

All hands on deck

Now it's time for a landmark in your piano playing—your first 'hands together' piece.

This will be the first time that you'll use both your left and right hands to play at the same time. Don't worry though—if you've worked through all the exercises for separate hands up to this point you shouldn't find this too difficult.

Look at the music example below.

The first thing to notice is that we now have notes appearing in both the treble clef (for the right hand) and in the bass clef (for the left hand). Don't be tempted to try to play through the piece with both hands right away! You'll be able to learn the piece much more quickly if you practice the left and right hands separately and become really familiar with them before you attempt to play 'hands together.'

Both hands start in their familiar five-finger positions; your right hand thumb should be on Middle C and your left hand little finger should be on the C an octave lower, as shown below:

Left Hand   Right Hand

First, try playing the right hand part on its own, starting with your thumb on Middle C. Count slowly and steadily making sure that you release the half note in bar 2 as you count 'three.' Then try exactly the same thing with the left hand, starting with your little finger on the C below Middle C.

> Did you notice anything when you played the left and right hand parts? If you listen carefully, you should notice that both the right and left hands are playing the same tune, but in different octaves.

Practice both the right and left hand parts until you know them really well. Ideally, you should be so familiar with them that you don't even need to look at the music, or at your hands. Once you're totally happy with both parts, then try putting them together. In this example the two hands don't ever play at exactly the same time, so start with the right hand part, counting through until you get to bar 3, where the left hand part begins, and swap back to the right hand in bar 5.

Congratulations! You've just played your first proper piano piece and you're well on the way to becoming a fully-fledged pianist. Let's keep the momentum going with another piece. Watch the left hand part closely here—it is no longer just copying what the right hand is doing!

And who says the right hand has to go first? Try this tune, which starts off in the bass clef:

Now let's up the pace again by including some eighth notes—remember to keep counting!

And finally, here's a lively piece with plenty of eighth notes and eighth note rests. Don't attempt this piece until you've totally mastered all the other examples in this chapter.

In this piece, the right hand imitates the left hand phrase, but it doesn't get it exactly right! See if you can spot the differences between what the left hand and right hand play. You should also try to get a sense of continuity between the two hands—as the tune moves from the bass clef to the treble clef in bar 3, try to make the transition as smooth as you can.

Hands together tips:

- The most important thing is to keep a steady rhythm. Don't worry if you play a wrong note; just keep going and keep the beat ticking away steadily.

- Try to match the volume between the two hands; one hand shouldn't be much louder than the other one.

- Start VERY slowly! It doesn't matter if it sounds ridiculously slow to start with; you can always speed up later.

Quiz answers from page 19

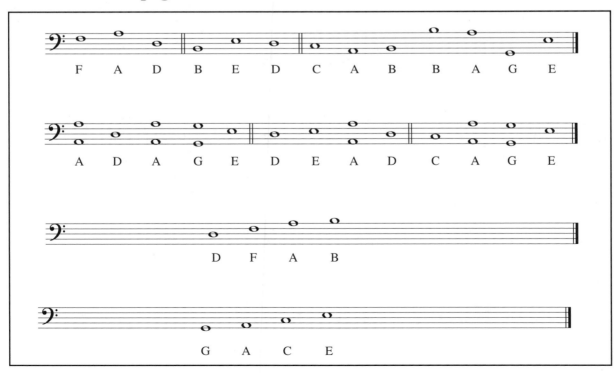

Chapter 9
Hands work together more

Although you've now played several pieces using both hands, you haven't yet played a piece where both hands are playing *at the same time*. That's all about to change now as we start to explore the sounds we can create when the left and right hands work together...

Let's start by looking at this simple piece:

Let's look at the left hand part first; it's extremely simple, and plays the same note on the first beat of every bar. This is good news because your right hand has a slightly more involved melody to play.

As always, start by practicing the left and right hands separately, making sure that you follow the fingering marked on the example. Only when you are satisfied that both parts are completely secure should you attempt to put them together.

Now we're going to liven up that left hand part a little, but don't panic—there's only one extra note to worry about!

Look out for bar 7—the left hand part changes from whole notes to half notes, so be ready to change notes more quickly. Try to lock in with the right hand part throughout, but especially in bar 7.

Everything on the 'one'

In music, the first beat of the bar is extremely important, and it generally receives more emphasis than any other beat. This is particularly true in the first example in this chapter, because beat one is the only time when you need to play notes with both your left and right hands at the same time.

Try really hard to hit both notes at exactly the same time, and with approximately the same force. If you can hear one note before the other, then slow down until the two notes blend into one.

Let's introduce a few more half notes into the left hand:

Once you've mastered this version, try adding quarter notes to the left hand part. Make sure that you practice the left hand separately before you attempt this hands together.

Look out for bar 7—apart from the first beat, the two hands don't play simultaneously at any point in this bar. Count very carefully and maintain the independence of the two hands (this is easier said than done, but persevere and eventually it will 'click').

Bar 7 is an example of a rhythmic technique known as *syncopation*, which involves the accenting of beats other than the first beat of the bar. Syncopation is used in all types of music, but it is particularly associated with jazz, pop and rock music. Once you've got it under your fingers, it's an incredibly enjoyble thing to play, so don't give up until you've mastered it!

Chapter 10
Introducing chords

By now you should be getting used to the sort of sounds you can create by playing hands together. One of the great things about the piano is that it is a *polyphonic* instrument—that is, it can play more than one note at a time. This enables pianists to create beautiful harmonies and *chords*, which is the technical term for several notes played at the same time.

By introducing chords into the left hand part, we can start to build up some great sounding sequences, as you'll see. Take a look at the example below, and pay special attention to the left hand part:

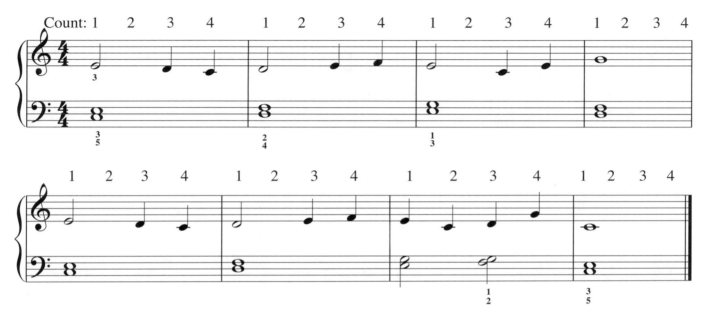

You should notice right away that where the left hand has previously been playing single notes, you now have two notes stacked on top of one another. In music notation this means that both notes are to be played at exactly the same time by the same hand.

Start by playing through the left hand part, but ignore the upper of the two notes. In this piece, it's more vital than ever that you use the suggested fingerings; the lower of the two numbers tells you which finger to use for the bottom note, so concentrate on that for the time being. Once you're happy with the bottom notes, play through the sequence again, focusing on the top notes. Only then should you attempt to play both notes together.

Here's another example of a simple melody in the right hand, supported by chords in the left hand:

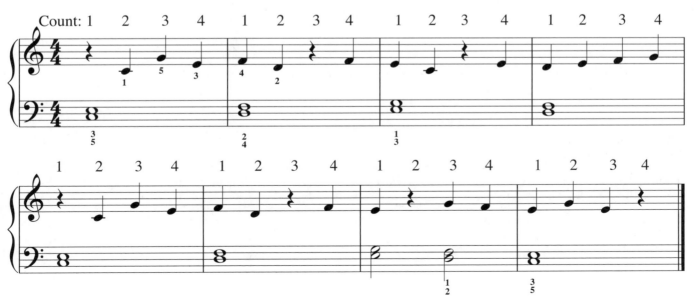

31

Now let's increase the speed of the chords in the left hand. Keep your wrist relaxed as you play through this example. If you feel your wrist and arm tensing up, it's a good idea to step away from the piano and let your arms swing loosely at your sides. Let your arm and wrist go completely limp and then shake them gently until the feeling of tenseness subsides. Playing with tight arms and wrists can permanently impair your playing so look out for it, especially when you're attempting something difficult or challenging.

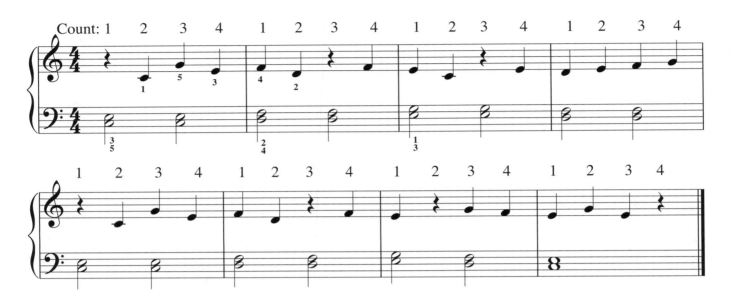

Finally, let's spice up the right hand melody with some eighth notes. If necessary, clap through the right hand part before you practice it, using the 'and method' to get all the eighth notes in the right places.

Look out for the tricky quarter note rest and quarter note chord in the left hand in bar 7. If necessary, isolate the left hand part in this bar and practice it separately.

Chord tips

Initially, you might find it difficult to get your left hand to press down the two notes in a chord at exactly the same time. Listen really carefully, and see if you can hear one note in the chord sounding before the other. If you can, then you're not playing the two notes together.

Aim for a really smooth transition from one chord to the next; only let go of the first chord a fraction of a second before you press down the next one.

32

Chapter 11
More chord power

In the last chapter we introduced the concept of a *chord* as more than one note played at the same time. You then played through several tunes using two-note chords in the left hand.

However, chords can get much more exciting than that, because there is no reason why we have to stop at chords with two notes. You can have chords with three, four, five or even eight notes, if you wish.

Here's a familiar melody from the last chapter, accompanied by three-note chords in the left hand.

As before, it's absolutely vital that you follow the suggested fingering for the left hand chords. If you don't you'll end up tying your hand in knots and it will be impossible to get a smooth progression from one chord to the next, which is what you should be aiming for.

All the chords you've played so far fall within the original five-note left hand position that you learned back in Chapter 5. However, to expand the harmonic possibilities open to us, we now need to introduce one new note.

Place your left hand in its usual five finger position, and play a chord with your little finger and thumb, like this:

As you know, these are the notes C and G, which are represented on the bass staff like this:

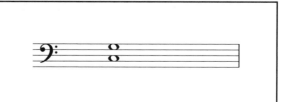

Now allow your little finger to slip down one note further, to the white key to the left of C, and play another chord, like this:

This new note is B, and is found on the bass clef here.

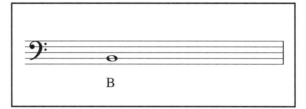

Practice moving between these two chords until you can do it without looking at your hands:

By adding one more note to each chord we can create a progession, which moves from here:

to here:

Practice moving between these two chords until you feel completely secure. Try to make the transition from one chord to the other as smooth as you can; remember that your thumb stays in the same place, while your little finger extends to reach the B note.

The progression that you've just played is one of the building blocks of all Western music, and can be found in all styles of music, from classical to jazz and pop. Let's put it to work under our familiar melody:

Your right hand isn't doing anything new here, so you should be free to concentrate on making your left hand chord transitions as smooth as possible. Look out for bar 7, where the pace of harmonic change quickens from whole notes to half notes.

Sometimes chords are broken up into their constituent notes, and spread throughout the bar, as in this example:

These are known as *broken chords* (this doesn't mean that they're defective in any way, just that the chord has been 'broken up' into its individual notes).

Whenever you see a passage of music that looks like this, you should always try to visualize the chord shapes as if they were 'unbroken' and all the notes were played at the same time. Try playing through the example above with your left hand, playing all the notes in each bar on the first beat. This will ensure that your hand is always in the correct position when you come to play the notes separately.

Here's a slightly more complicated example of the same technique. Try playing through this simple sequence with block chords in the left hand:

Practice until your left hand is comfortable with the chord shapes and the right hand melody is secure. Then try this version, which introduces some eighth note movement into the bass part, while maintaining the same basic chord 'shapes.'

This left hand figuration is similar to the 'Alberti' pattern you learned back on page 24, and is another very common accompaniment style in classical music.

As you play these eighth note passages, resist the temptation to allow any of the notes to 'hang on' longer than they should. You should never find yourself playing more than one note at a time (until you come to the final chord in bar 8, of course). Be very deliberate as you raise each finger and aim for an even tone, with no one note significantly louder or softer than any of the others.

Think ahead!

When reading music, it's a really good idea to get into the habit of always looking ahead to the next few bars. This will give you a chance to prepare for anything that's coming up over the musical horizon.

In the piece above, you don't have anything to play after the third beat of the bar. So, use beats 3 and 4 to look ahead to the next bar and prepare yourself mentally for what's coming up. Look at the notes the right hand is going to play and the position that your left hand will need to be in, and be prepared!

Now let's make the right hand melody more interesting by adding in some quarter notes. The left hand part stays the same:

And finally, here's a stamina test for your left hand! This piece has continuous eighth note movement in the left hand for over six bars, and it will really feel like hard work to start with:

Don't be put off by the sight of all those eighth notes—remember that the underlying chord shapes are still the same, so your left hand is still changing position at the same rate. As always, isolate the left hand and practice really slowly and steadily. Make sure that the rhythm of the eighth notes is as even as you can get it before you start to speed up.

Count for yourself

From this point on, we're not going to print the counts above each music example, as you've now encountered all the different rhythmic patterns that we're using in this book.

However, that doesn't mean that you should stop counting yourself; keep counting, whether out loud, or in your head, until your sense of the beat is absolutely rock solid. If you find yourself 'losing' the beat, then practice with a metronome. Gradually this sense of the underlying pulse of the music will become second nature to you, but until it does, keep on counting!

Chapter 12
Changing position

Up to this point your right hand has been restricted to playing five notes, with the thumb anchored to Middle C. Now it's time to set your right hand free and allow it to roam around the keyboard to discover some new notes.

In fact, there are three new notes that we'd like to introduce you to, which can be found above the five-finger position that you're already familiar with:

On the staff, these notes are represented like this:

So, how are we going to reach these new notes? Simple—by moving the right hand to new five-finger positions, higher up the keyboard.

Take a look at this example. The first phrase should be easy for you to play, as it's based around the familiar five-finger position, with your thumb on Middle C. The second phrase uses exactly the same fingers, but starts on E instead of C.

Notice that you have a half note rest at the end of bar 2; this should give you enough time to move your hand into its new position. Here's how to do it:

As soon as you've released the first note in bar 2 (on the third beat), move your thumb up so that it's right next to where your fourth finger was:

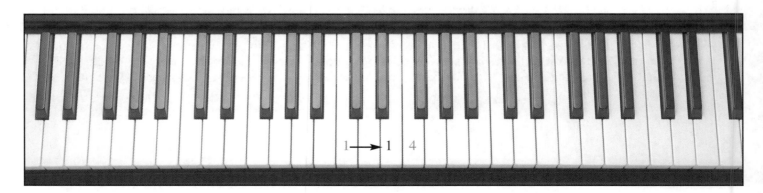

Once your thumb is in position on E, then let your other four fingers cover the four white notes to the right:

You're now in the correct position to play bars 3 and 4.

When you reach the end of bar 4, you need to do exactly the same thing again. As soon as you've finished playing the A half note with your fourth finger, move your thumb up to the white note below it:

Hey, presto! Your hand is now in a new five-finger position with the thumb on G, and you can now finish bars 5 and 6 of the music example:

Your index finger is now covering the new note A, your middle finger will be used to play B and your ring finger should fall on the C an octave above Middle C.

Musical phrases

You'll often hear musicians talking about musical *phrases*. This is an example of the similarities between music and language; just like a sentence in English, melodies are almost always divided into smaller sub-sections called phrases. In the previous example, each phrase lasts for two bars, and is divided from the next one by a half note rest.

As you practice this example make sure that, at the end of each phrase (in the half note rest), you get your thumb into its new position as quickly as you can, so that you are prepared to start the next two-bar phrase right on time. The half note rest is longer than you think, so count out loud. There is often a temptation to rush through rests and get straight on with the next notes—don't forget that rests give music time to 'breathe,' and are vital to creating a convincing melody. Imagine trying to sing a tune that doesn't have any breaks to take a breath, and you'll get a good idea of the effect of rushing through rests.

39

Let's look at another example and investigate another way for you to move your right hand into its new positions:

This example is very similar to the previous one in that it consists of two-bar phrases in different positions on the keyboard. Look at the last note of the first phrase (in bar 2) and the first note of the second phrase (in bar 3)—they're the same.

This makes it really easy to move from one position to the next. In the half note rest in bar 2, simply move your thumb up so that it's resting on the same note that you just played with your third finger, like this:

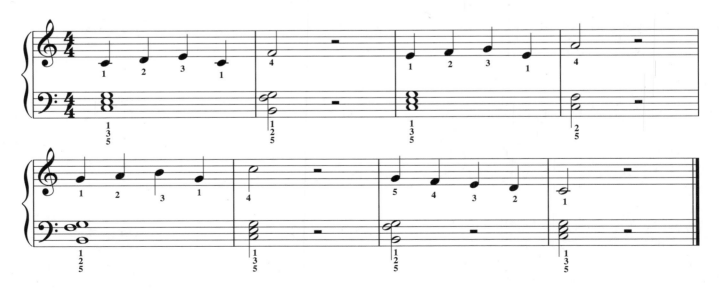

Move your third finger out of the way at the last minute, to make room for your thumb, and you'll be ready to play the next phrase.

After you've played the third phrase (bars 5-6), you need to return to your starting position to play the last phrase. There are no guide fingers here to help you, so you'll just have to remember where Middle C is and get your thumb back there in the two beats of rest before the start of bar 7.

Now let's try putting these new notes and positions to work in a hands-together piece. All the right hand fingerings are marked below the notes—make sure you stick to them:

Once again, remember not to rush through the rests; count slowly and steadily and come in precisely on time on the first beat of the next bar.

Chapter 13
More new notes

A new note for the left hand

In this penultimate chapter, we're going to introduce a couple of new notes for your left and right hands, before moving on to the grand finale in Chapter 14.

Let's start with a new note for the left hand; it sits on the top line of the staff, and is called A.

In the same way that you extended your little finger downwards to reach the low B, you can extend your thumb upwards from its standard five-finger position to find this new note, as shown below:

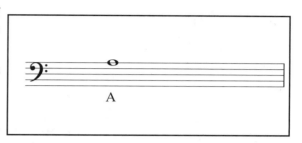

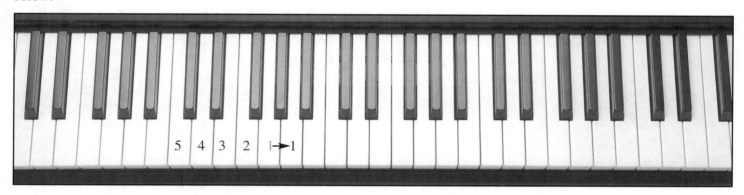

Play a chord with the thumb and little finger of your left hand on G and C (as shown below) and practice extending your thumb up to the next white note to find A:

Here's a short piece to put this new note to work. It first appears in bar 3, and again in bar 7, so isolate those sections and practice them separately, before attempting the piece hands together:

41

A new note for the right hand

You may recall that on page 7 we mentioned that the black keys on the piano were called *sharps* or *flats*. The time has now come to add one of these notes to your collection.

The note we have chosen lies in between the white notes F and G and is called F sharp (this is sometimes written as F♯).

The sharp symbol tells us to play the next highest note on the keyboard from the letter name before the symbol. So, if we start at F, the next highest note (moving up the keyboard to the right), is the black key in between F and G.

Experiment with playing F and F♯ together at the same time; it's not a very nice noise, is it?

That's because F and F♯ are very close to one another in pitch; in fact, they're as close as any two notes can ever be on the piano, so when you play them together the sounds 'fight' with one another. Although this can sound unpleasant in isolation, it's actually a very useful musical technique, which can be used in composition and is known as *dissonance*.

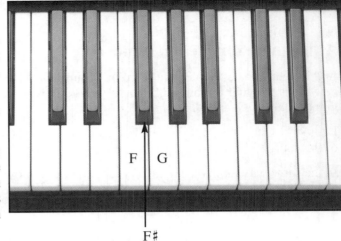

Let's take a look at how we represent the note of F♯ on the staff:

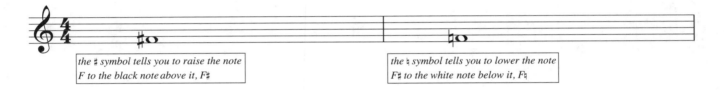

the ♯ symbol tells you to raise the note F to the black note above it, F♯

the ♮ symbol tells you to lower the note F♯ to the white note below it, F♮

We simply add the ♯ (sharp) symbol in front of the note F to create F♯. In musical notation the effect of a sharp lasts for one bar only; after that all Fs will revert to their former state, which is known as F *natural*, and is given the sign ♮. In fact, all the Fs you've played up to this point could have been described as F naturals, but for the sake of convenience we only use the word *natural* when there is any possibility of ambiguity.

This new note opens up all sorts of exciting musical possibilities, so let's go ahead and put it to use.

This example combines right hand position changes, as discussed in the previous chapter, with our new note, F♯.

In this example, the half note rests have been removed, so you're going to have to be much quicker at moving from one position to the next; as soon as you have played the last note in bar 2, start moving your thumb up so that it's poised in position to play the E on the first beat of bar 3.

Let's take a closer look at bars 6 and 7. If you've followed the position changes correctly up to this point, you should reach the first beat of bar 6 with your third finger playing the quarter note B and your index finger playing the A, bringing you to rest on the G note with your thumb.

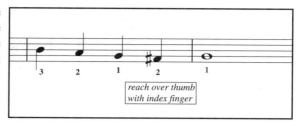

So far, so good, but how are we going to reach that elusive F♯ black note?

Very simply, all you need to do is reach over the top of your thumb with your index finger to press down the F♯, as shown below:

You can then finish the piece with your thumb resting on the note G. It's very important that you don't use any other finger to play the F♯—if you do, you could drag your hand out of position, and find that you don't have a convenient finger to finish the piece with.

Let's add a left hand accompaniment to this melody—listen out for the bright effect of the F♯:

Sharps and flats

Back at the beginning of the book, we mentioned that the black notes could be described either as *sharps* or *flats*. The generic term for these is *accidentals,* which is slightly misleading as, most of the time, they are placed in music very deliberately.

You've now encountered your first black note, in the form of F♯, but you may be wondering why we haven't introduced any *flats*. This is because sharps and flats can be used as different ways of describing the same note. Just as a sharp tells the pianist to use the next highest note on the keyboard, so a flat tells you to use the next *lowest*.

So, if we were to start on the note G, and move down the keyboard (left) to the next lowest note, we would also come to the same black note that we have called F♯. Hence, this note can also be called G flat, or G♭ . However, it's more typical to use F♯, so that's what we've done in this book.

Chapter 14
Let's play!

So, after several weeks of hard work, you're finally ready to learn your first ever piano piece. Turn to the last page in this book and take a look at it—it looks just like a real piece of music, and that's because it is!

Although this piece takes up a whole page of music, it's actually made up of three sections, which we'll look at individually. Here's the first of the three sections:

Section 1

The first thing to notice about this piece is that the first bar seems to be very short! It only contains two eighth notes, whereas a full bar would normally contain eight (as in the left hand in the following bar).

This effectively means that the piece starts on the fourth beat of the bar. It just so happens that all the exercises you've played so far have started on the first beat of the bar, but there's no particular reason why a tune can't start on any beat of the bar. In fact, it's very common for melodies to start on the fourth beat, as a lead-in to the first beat of the next bar. Musicians call this a *pickup*.

In order to get these two notes in the right place, you're going to need to count yourself in very carefully. Try the exercise below; count steadily from one to three and then play these three notes as you count '4 and 1':

You can imagine there is a three-beat rest in front of the two eighth notes—the only reason that it's not shown on the music is that it's empty space. Every time you play this piece, count the first three beats in your head before you come in.

Whatever you do, don't count 'one' as you play the first note, otherwise the rest of the piece is going to get very confusing! Try to get used to the sound of saying 'four and one' as you start the piece.

Now try playing this short example:

The left hand comes in on the first beat of the bar (as you count 'four and **one**'). Try to make sure that the right and left hands hit their notes at exactly the same time.

Now take a look at bar 6 (when we count bars, we ignore the pick up bar, so bar 6 is the second bar on the second line of music).

The first two notes in this bar are right hand chords. So far, all the chords you've played have been in the left hand, but there's no reason why the right hand can't join in the fun.

Let's start by practicing some simple chords in the Middle C five-finger position:

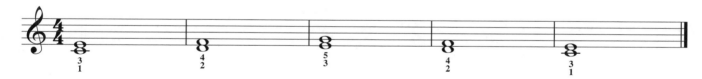

Follow the fingering shown under each chord and you shouldn't have to move your hand from its customary position.

Now let's try some similar chords in different positions on the keyboard:

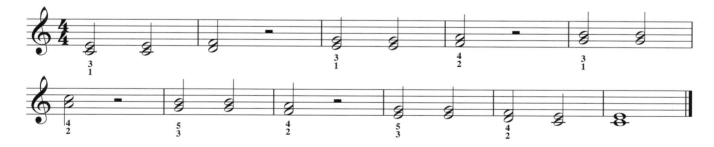

Each set of three chords uses a different five-finger position, as follows:
Bars 1-2: Thumb on Middle C
Bars 3-4: Thumb on E
Bars 5-6: Thumb on G
Bars 7-8: Thumb on E
Bars 9-11: Thumb on Middle C

Now you're ready to experience the incredible sound of chords in both the left and right hands:

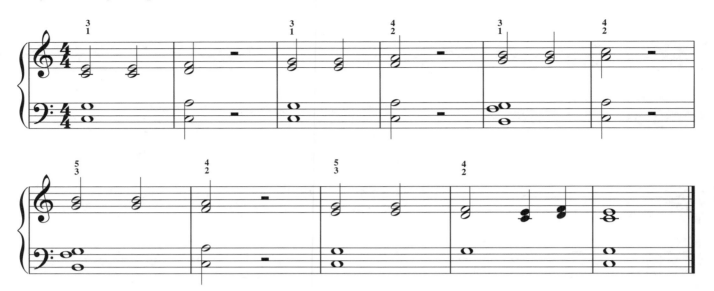

At some points in this piece you'll be playing five notes at once! Enjoy the rich, warm sound that this generates, and really try to get all of the notes to sound exactly at the same time.

Now let's take a look at our final piece once again.

In the bar before the right hand chords, you may have noticed a large leap in the melody, from Middle C to the C an octave above.

You should be quite used to moving your right hand around the keyboard by now, and even though this leap is bigger than anything you've attempted so far, exactly the same principles apply. The last three notes in the phrase above can be played easily with the right hand in a five-finger position with the thumb on F. The first four notes can be played easily in your 'home' position with the thumb on Middle C.

Therefore the only issue is: how do we get from one to the other? The answer, as ever, is **practice**!

Start by playing the first four notes, ending with your thumb on Middle C. Then move your whole hand so that your little finger is resting on the C an octave higher. Get used to the feeling of distance between the two hand positions and try to remember it. Keep doing this over and over again until you can find the upper C with your little finger really quickly (you can even try doing it with your eyes closed). Eventually, your brain will develop what's called a *muscle memory* of the correct positions and you'll be able to go straight there.

This short exercise will help you:

46

Section 2

Section 2 is a quieter, more reflective passage that contrasts with the busy eighth notes of Section 1. This is a common technique in music of all genres—our ears (and brains) like to hear contrasts in mood, tempo and harmony as a piece progresses. It prevents the music from becoming boring and keeps our interest up.

With that in mind, let's take a look at this eight-bar section:

The right hand starts in a five-finger position with the thumb on E and stays there until bar 6 of this section.

When you reach the last quarter note of bar 6, you will need to move your thumb up to G, so you can reach the top C with your ring finger. Look out for the F♯ at the end of bar 7 and remember the 'index finger over the top' maneuver from the previous chapter.

The last two eighth notes of bar 8 are a pickup into Section 3.

Notice how different this section of music looks, with its many half notes and rests—it's a chance for the piece to calm down a bit after all the action of Section 1. Try to get this feeling across when you play it—perhaps you could try to play Section 2 more quietly, returning to full volume when you reach Section 3.

Section 3

The great thing about Section 3 of this piece is that it's almost an exact repeat of Section 1, so there's no more new music to learn. The only thing that differs is the final chord of the piece—look carefully at it and you should see a wavy vertical line stretching all the way from the bottom note to the top. This is called an *arpeggio,* and it means that you should spread the notes of the chord rapidly from bottom to top, instead of playing them all at the same time. Try it—it's a lot of fun!

All that remains is for you to practice all of the examples in this chapter thoroughly before attempting the final piece on the next page.

The final frontier

We've now given you all the tools you need to play this final piece; it's up to you to practice diligently and put all these little bits together until you've mastered it.

One final hint—if you're finding it difficult to motivate yourself to practice enough to get over this final hurdle, then set yourself a deadline that you can't avoid. Invite some friends over to hear you play in a couple of weeks, or tell your family to be ready for a performance at the weekend. That way you've got something to aim for, and a reason to practice.

We wish you every success in your future as a pianist—get out there and explore all the wonderful music that is now available to you, from classical greats to jazz and pop. Continue to improve your technique, knowledge of music theory and notation and you can look forward to many years of musical pleasure from this incredible instrument.

Etude

Moderately

Mike Sheppard